The Prohibition of Domestic Violence in Islam

The Prohibition of Domestic Violence in Islam

A Fatwa Issued By
Shaykh M. Hisham Kabbani
and Dr. Homayra Ziad

Published By
World Organization for Resource Development and Education
www.worde.org

Published and Distributed by:

World Organization for Resource Development and Education (WORDE)
1875 I Street NW, Suite 500
Washington, DC 20006
Tel: (202) 595-1355
Fax: (202) 318-2582
Email: staff@worde.org
Web: www.worde.org

First Edition: July 2011
THE PROHIBITION OF DOMESTIC VIOLENCE IN ISLAM
ISBN: 978-1-930409-97-2

Library of Congress Cataloging-in-Publication Data

Kabbani, Muhammad Hisham.
The prohibition of domestic violence in Islam / a fatwa Issued by Shaykh M. Hisham Kabbani and Dr. Homayra Ziad.
p. cm.
Includes bibliographical references.
ISBN 978-1-930409-97-2 (alk. paper)
1. Family violence (Islamic law) 2. Women (Islamic law) 3. Women--Violence against. 4. Fatwas. I. Ziad, Homayra. II. Title.
KBP4187.K33 2011
297.5'63--dc23

2011027306

PRINTED IN THE UNITED STATES OF AMERICA
15 14 13 12 11 05 06 07 08 09

Table of Contents

About the Publisher i

About the Authors iii

Publisher's Notes v

Introduction 1

Qur'an and Ḥadīth: Founts of Guidance 2
Our Approach 4

Interpreting the Holy Qur'an 5

The Socio-historical Context of Revelation 5
Verse 4:34 in the Context of Broader Qur'anic Humanism 8

A Linguistic Exploration of the Word "*Ḍaraba*" 13

Interpreting the Qur'an through the Qur'an 13
Ten Qur'anic Meanings of "*Ḍaraba*" 15
Other Interpretations 17

The Importance of Prophet Muhammad's Example 21

Prophet Muhammad's High Regard for Women 21

Conclusion 27

Appendix: Verses That Use the Verb "*Ḍaraba*" 29

Glossary of Islamic Terms 39

About the Publisher

The World Organization for Resource Development and Education (WORDE) is a nonprofit educational organization whose mission is to enhance communication and understanding between Muslim and non-Muslim communities and to strengthen Muslim institutions that will mitigate social and political conflict.

WORDE shapes public policy by cultivating a better understanding of Islamic ideologies that promote pluralism and service to humanity, while exposing the roots of extremism that disrupt the peaceful coexistence of societies everywhere.

WORDE Specialists are academics, theologians, development experts and policy analysts who develop effective, long-term solutions in the key areas of educational reform, resource development, and international security. Many of them serve as advisers to various US government agencies as well as international organizations and governments around the world.

About the Authors

Shaykh Muhammad Hisham Kabbani

Shaykh Kabbani is a renowned religious scholar of both traditional Islamic law and the spiritual science of Sufism. He hails from a respected family of traditional Islamic scholars, which includes the former head of the Association of Muslim Scholars of Lebanon and the present grand mufti (highest Islamic religious authority) of Lebanon. For three decades he has promoted traditional Islamic principles of peace, love, compassion and social cohesion, while rigorously opposing extremism. As deputy leader of the Naqshbandi Haqqani Sufi Order, he is authorized to issue religious edicts and counsel the students of the movement, which by recent reports number in the millions.

Since the early 1990s, Shaykh Kabbani has been pivotal in helping non-Muslim societies understand the difference between moderate mainstream Muslims and minority extremist sects.

In 2010, the shaykh hosted HRH the Prince of Wales and has previously hosted two international conferences in the U.S. and various regional conferences around the world. His counsel is sought by journalists, academics, policymakers, and by community leaders and activists who turn to him for guidance and support.

In the United States, Shaykh Kabbani serves as Chairman, Islamic Supreme Council of America; Founder, Naqshbandi Sufi Order of America; Advisor, World Organization for Resource Development and Education; and Chairman, As-Sunnah Foundation of America. In the United Kingdom, Shaykh Kabbani is founder of the Centre for Spiritual and Cultural Advancement and was lead scholar for the Sufi Muslim Council, a non-profit NGO that consults to the British government on public policy and social and religious issues.

Shaykh Kabbani has written numerous books on Islamic spirituality. He is well known in policy development circles and has presented several critical position papers on the current state of global Islam, counter-terrorism, and the primacy of democratic principles in Islam.

Dr. Homayra Ziad

Dr. Ziad is Assistant Professor of Religion at Trinity College, where she teaches courses on Islam. Her scholarly interests include intellectual and cultural trends in Muslim South Asia, theoretical and practical Sufism, theologies of pluralism, and Qur'anic hermeneutics.

Dr. Ziad earned a Ph.D. in Islamic Studies and an M.A. in International Relations from Yale University, and a B.A. in Economics from Bryn Mawr College. She has published on the Naqshbandi revivalism of the eighteenth-century Delhi theologian and poet Khwajah Mir Dard, Urdu literature and *qawwali*, women and Islam, chaplaincy and Scriptural Reasoning, interfaith work, and Muslim liberation theology. She is a member of the Islam steering committee of the American Academy of Religion.

Dr. Ziad worked as an Associate at the Chaplain's Office at Yale and was also the editor of *Chowrangi*, a quarterly magazine devoted to the dissemination of progressive Pakistani and Pakistani-American voices. She has been a resource on topics related to Islam for media outlets such as Voice of America, BBC Radio Asian Network, *The Boston Globe*, *India New England*, and *Jane Magazine*. She is a featured scholar on the popular Islamic website, eShaykh.com.

Dr. Ziad has organized and participated in interfaith initiatives and educational outreach on faith. In this capacity, she is involved in the practice of Scriptural Reasoning and is on the Board of Advisors of the Scriptural Reasoning Society. She also works on Jewish-Muslim interfaith dialogue with the Reconstructionist Rabbinical College in Philadelphia, Pennsylvania, and at Hebrew College in Newton Centre, Massachusetts.

Publisher's Notes

This booklet is directed to those who seek to understand the historic and religious aspects of domestic violence among Muslims. Where Arabic texts are crucial to the discussion, we have included their English translations and textual citations. For readers familiar with Arabic and Islamic teachings, for further clarity please consult the cited sources.

Translations from Arabic to English pose unique challenges which we have tried our best to make understandable to Western readers. Quotes from the Holy Qur'an and the Holy Traditions of Prophet Muhammad *(āḥadīth)* are offset and cited. Where gender-specific pronouns such as "he" and "him" are applied in a general sense, no discrimination is intended towards women, upon whom The Almighty bestowed great honor.

It is important to understand that Islamic teachings are primarily based on four sources, in this order:

- **Holy Qur'an**: The holy book of divine revelation (God's Word) granted to Prophet Muhammad. Reference to Holy Qur'an appears as "4:12," indicating "Chapter 4, Verse 12."
- **Sunnah**: Holy traditions of Prophet Muhammad; the systematic recording of his words and actions that comprise the *ḥadīth*. For fifteen centuries, Islam has applied a strict, highly technical standard of rating each narration in terms of its authenticity and categorizing its line of "transmission." As this book is not highly technical, we simplified the reporting of *ḥadīth*, but included the narrator and source texts to support the discussion at hand.
- ***Ijma'***: The adherence or agreement of the experts of independent reasoning *(āhl al-ijtihād)* to the conclusions of a given ruling pertaining to what is permitted and what is forbidden after the passing of the Prophet, peace be upon him, as well as the agreement of the Community of Muslims concerning what is obligatorily known of the religion with its decisive proofs. Perhaps a clearer statement of this principle is: "We do not separate (in belief and practice) from the largest group of the Muslims."

- **Legal Rulings:** Highly trained Islamic scholars form legal rulings, "*fatawa*," from their interpretation of the Qur'an and the Sunnah, known as *ijtihād*. Such rulings are intended to provide Muslims an Islamic context regarding contemporary social norms. In theological terms, scholars who form legal opinions have completed many years of rigorous training and possess degrees similar to a doctorate in divinity in Islamic knowledge, or in legal terms, hold the status of a high court or supreme court judge, or higher.

Please note, the universally recognized salutation, *ṣallAllāhu ʿalayhi wa sallam*, "God's blessings and greetings of peace be upon him," is commonly recited after the holy name of Prophet Muhammad, represented in this text as "(s)." While this frequent occurrence may seem tedious, it is deeply appreciated by Muslim readers.

Introduction

"Are Muslim men allowed to beat their wives?"

This question is not an unexpected one; after all, Islam and violence is a hot-button issue in Western public discourse. But what is surprising to us is how often it is a Muslim who poses this question. Many Muslims, both Western and non-Western, feel betrayed by intellectuals and scholars who continue to insist on simplistic, dogmatic edicts in response to complex issues. An Islamic ruling on this contentious subject must be consonant with classical understandings while addressing the normative values of today's global civilization.

Islamic jurisprudence upholds the values of mercy, compassion and love in the conduct of family affairs. Today, extremists are leading a concerted effort to erode these values. In fact, certain contemporary scholars have issued rulings that accept spousal abuse as an acceptable practice, based on a narrow interpretation of a particular Qur'anic verse that ostensibly permits the striking of wives as a last resort response to "disobedience." By decontextualizing Qur'anic statements and disregarding centuries of Islamic jurisprudence, they have skewed the public perception of Islamic family law. It is not surprising then that increasing numbers of Muslims and non-Muslims believe that Islamic law sanctions men to beat their wives.

To remain relevant to the human experience, legal rulings must adapt to changing societal circumstances and norms, while upholding the core Qur'anic values of mercy and justice. Instead of blindly following in the footsteps of previous literalist interpretations, it is time for Muslim scholars to strive for novel interpretations based on classical methodologies. This is not thinking outside the box; rather, it is extending the boundaries of the box in which we think.

Qur'an and Ḥadīth: Founts of Guidance

The Qur'an continues to exercise paramount authority in the lives of Muslims. Revealed to the Prophet Muhammad (s) over a period of twenty-three years by the Archangel Gabriel, Muslims consider the Qur'an the literal Word of God, unaltered and unedited. It is not only a book of inspirational value, but a book of practical guidance and law in a myriad of affairs, including marital relations.

Second only in importance to the Qur'an are the actions and words of the Prophet Muhammad (s) throughout the twenty-three years in which he received revelation. These reports about the Prophet (s) from his companions and family are known as *ḥadīth*. The sound *ḥadīth* are a body of texts whose authenticity and authorship have been accepted by the early scholars of Islam, and they are a source for rulings on matters of law, similar to the Qur'an. Additionally, the *ḥadīth* often provide interpretations of Qur'anic verses or other details necessary to derive legal rulings.

Rulings about the notion of "wife-beating" in Islam revolve around only a single verse of the Holy Qur'an (4:34). The verse in question follows below, along with two typical translations:

الرِّجَالُ قَوَّامُونَ عَلَى النِّسَاءِ بِمَا فَضَّلَ اللَّهُ بَعْضَهُمْ عَلَى بَعْضٍ وَبِمَا أَنفَقُوا مِنْ
أَمْوَالِهِمْ فَالصَّالِحَاتُ قَانِتَاتٌ حَافِظَاتٌ لِّلْغَيْبِ بِمَا حَفِظَ اللَّهُ وَاللاَّتِي تَخَافُونَ
نُشُوزَهُنَّ فَعِظُوهُنَّ وَاهْجُرُوهُنَّ فِي الْمَضَاجِعِ وَاضْرِبُوهُنَّ فَإِنْ أَطَعْنَكُمْ فَلاَ
تَبْغُوا عَلَيْهِنَّ سَبِيلاً إِنَّ اللَّهَ كَانَ عَلِيًّا كَبِيرًا

Men are the protectors and maintainers of women, because Allah has given the one more (strength) than the other, and because they support them from their means. Therefore, the righteous women are devoutly obedient and guard in (the husband's) absence what Allah would have them guard. As to those women on whose part you fear disloyalty and ill conduct, (first) admonish them; (next) refuse to share their beds; (and last) beat them (lightly). But if they return to obedience, seek not against them means (of annoyance), for Allah is Most High, Great (above you all).

(A. Yusuf Ali)[1]

[1] Sūratu 'n-Nisā' (Women), 4:34, A. Yusuf Ali, The Holy Qur'an: Text, Translation and Commentary.

Men are in charge of women, because Allah has made the one of them to excel the other, and because they spend of their property (for the support of women). So good women are the obedient, guarding in secret that which Allah has guarded. As for those from whom you fear rebellion, admonish them and banish them to beds apart, and scourge them. Then if they obey you, seek not a way against them. Lo! Allah is ever High, Exalted, Great.

(Muhammad Marmaduke Pickthall) [2]

Within this verse, one word invokes intense controversy: *w'aḍribūhunna,* from the Arabic verb "*ḍaraba.*" Based on this one word, many contemporary scholars assert that a man may beat his wife. For example, Indian scholar Shahul Hameed writes on IslamOnline.net:

> *Some scholars argue that the word in this context does not mean "beat" or "hit"; it means just "leave (them)." But it is obvious, and Allah knows best, that the word stands here for "punishment"....* [3]

Usually, such scholars qualify the verb "beat" by the adverb "lightly," as in the above translation by Yusuf Ali, to mitigate the harshness of the punishment they perceive in this verse. However, even this translation is misleading because it reinforces a faulty assumption that the Quran stipulates any form of physical violence towards one's spouse.

---

[2] Sūratu 'n-Nisā' (Women), 4:34, Muhammad Marmaduke Pickthall, *The Meaning of the Glorious Qur'an.* Unless otherwise noted, all subsequent Qur'anic translations in this paper are from the Pickthall text.

3http://www.islamonline.net/servlet/Satellite?cid=1123996220182&pagename=IslamOnline- English-AAbout_Islam%2FAAboutIslamCounselorE%2FAAboutIslamCounselorE, as referenced on July 2, 2006.

> We emphasize a different aspect of our tradition that reflects mercy and justice in today's world. While tapping a wife with a toothstick was considered gentle where violence against women was previously acceptable, in fact there is no place for physical punishment of a wife, however gentle.

Our Approach

In our analysis, we present a number of alternative and linguistically valid interpretations of the above-mentioned verse of Qur'an. We also appeal to *ḥadīth* that privilege an understanding of spousal relations and spousal abuse consonant with contemporary norms. We do recognize the existence of some *ḥadīth* that seem to accept the word *ḍaraba* as 'strike' (at the same time, these *ḥadīth* also express great discomfort with this interpretation, and soften its implications by limiting physical chastisement to a symbolic tap of a *miswāk* (twig used as a toothbrush) or handkerchief). It is important to note that we do not reject these *ḥadīth* as false or falsely attributed; rather, we believe that the message must have been appropriate to the particular context in which the Prophet (s) was speaking (suitable to the historical context and prevalent cultural practices). Rather than rejecting the content, we are emphasizing a different aspect of our vast interpretive tradition that is consonant with mercy and justice in today's world. While tapping a wife with a *miswāk* may have been just and gentle in a context where harsh violence against women had previously been culturally acceptable, in our contemporary context there is no place for physical punishment, however gentle, of a wife. We are not rejecting those *ḥadīth* that appear to state otherwise, but rather emphasizing the myriad of others that predicate marriage on mercy, love and mutual support.

Interpreting the Holy Qur'an

A comprehensive approach to understanding problematic Qur'anic verses requires deep scholarship, seeking not only the reason a verse was revealed and what events transpired in connection with its revelation, but a genuine understanding of the intent behind that revelation, command of the classical Arabic language of the Qur'an and often a knowledge of the various dialects used in the different areas in which the Qur'an was revealed (for each tribe's usage of a word might have differed from that of others). One must also consider how the Prophet (s) and his Companions often explained a verse of the Qur'an in a manner quite different from the apparent meaning of the text. It takes an expert in linguistics to understand all the meanings in a verse, both explicit and inferred.

Moreover, the Qur'an frequently uses allegories suited to all readers: young and old, male and female. The Qur'an can be deliberately broad, using allusive rather than direct language when discussing issues that may need to be accessed at several different levels of understanding, consonant with the preparedness and receptivity of the reader. It is for just this reason that classical scholars insist that the deeper meanings of the Holy Qur'an can only be accessed through a knowledgeable scholar, well-versed in such subtleties.

The Socio-historical Context of Revelation

To reach a thorough understanding of the verse in question, we must also examine the context of its revelation. We must consider the verse both in its historical context, and in the broader context of the Qur'anic message of humanism. The Qur'an was revealed in a social context in which spousal abuse, murder and even infanticide were commonplace. God gave the Prophet Muhammad (s) the charge to establish a new rule of law, transforming a clannish society into a highly civilized community in which the rights of both men and women should be respected at all levels of individual and societal conduct.

This particular verse must be seen in the context of the social norms of pre-Islamic Arabia. The concept of women's rights did not exist, women were considered chattel, and treated like slaves. A wife's alleged

misbehavior often resulted in a brutal beating, isolation, or starvation and sometimes even death. Men were rarely held accountable for their actions against their spouses. With the Qur'anic revelation, Muslims were taught that there is no distinction between a Muslim man and woman in faith: both have the same rights and obligations, and are promised equal rewards in heaven. The Qur'an brought a transformative message of mercy and spiritual equality to a society that had very little understanding of such norms.

Sexually promiscuous behavior was also commonplace. The Qur'an sought to restrict the expression of sexuality within the bounds of marriage and prevent all the concomitant dangers of adultery, such as disease and unwanted pregnancy. Therefore, in verse 4:34, some classical scholars have understood "disloyalty and ill conduct (*nushūz*)" on the part of the wife to refer not to mere disobedience, but to sexual infidelity.[4]

The Prophet (s) said:

فخطب الناس وقال ... ولكم عليهن أن لا يوطئن فرشكم أحدا تكرهونه.

It is your right that they do not make friends with anyone of whom you do not approve, and never commit adultery.[5]

It is in this context that the verse applies. As in all teachings of the Prophet (s), a step-by-step process is followed in correcting wrong behavior. In revealing the rules and practices of Islam to the Prophet (s),

[4] "The term *nushūz* (lit., "rebellion," but here rendered as "ill will") comprises every kind of deliberate bad behavior of a wife towards her husband or of a husband towards his wife, including what is nowadays described as "mental cruelty;" with reference to the husband, it also denotes "ill treatment," in the physical sense, of his wife (cf. verse 128 of this sūrah)." Muhammad Asad, tr., *The Message of the Qur'an* (Gibraltar: Dar al Andalus, 1980), 109.

[5] Muslim b. al-Hajjāj al-Qushayrī, Saḥīḥ Muslim, second edition, Book of Hajj, Section "Hajj of the Prophet", ed. Maḥmūd Fu'ād 'Abd al-Bāqī (Beirut: Dār Iḥyā' al-Turāth al-'Arābī, 1978), No. 1218, retrieved August 30, 2010 from http://www.al-eman.com/islamlib/viewchp.asp?BID=138&CID=68&SW.

God never expected new forms of behavior to be adopted instantly, but always took a multi-stage approach. We can see this in the way in which relations between men and women were gradually modified over the twenty-three years in which the Qur'an was revealed. At first, the topic of sexual relations was not addressed and men and women were not prevented from engaging in the sexual practices commonplace in pre-Islamic Arabia. In time, the Qur'an began to encourage marriage, and simultaneously proscribed adultery and fornication. This was followed by gradually restricting behavior that might lead to sexual impropriety. Accordingly, we can see that the intent of the verse in question is to prevent behavior on the woman's part that would destroy the foundation of the marriage. An equivalent verse addressing the man's behavior is 4:128:

وَإِنِ امْرَأَةٌ خَافَتْ مِن بَعْلِهَا نُشُوزًا أَوْ إِعْرَاضًا فَلَا جُنَاحَ عَلَيْهِمَا أَن
يُصْلِحَا بَيْنَهُمَا صُلْحًا وَالصُّلْحُ خَيْرٌ

If a woman fears ill treatment from her husband, or desertion,
it is no sin for them twain if they make terms of peace
between themselves. Peace is better.[6]

If we examine the broader history of human civilization we see that, in most cases, societies tend to evolve over time. Europe's transition from the Middle Ages to the Renaissance is a case in point. Recognizing this historical reality, the Qur'an specified a code of behavior that restricted a number of societal practices that prevailed at the time of its revelation while, at the same time, leaving the door open for future scholars to adapt the code to new and different social conditions. Understanding this methodology will help us to appreciate the ability of the religion to function in every age and situation.

---

[6] Sūratu 'n-Nisā' (Women), 4:128.

> The Qur'an specified a code of behavior that restricted some societal practices while leaving the door open for future scholars to adapt the code to new and different social conditions.

Verse 4:34 in the Context of Broader Qur'anic Humanism

Islam has always upheld the highest standard of morality and ethics when it comes to human relations. To further understand the context of verse 4:34, we must examine the importance of family in the Qur'an, both as it relates to the individual and to society as a whole. We must also consider what God says about the relationship between husbands and wives.

The Qur'an is intent on protecting and upholding family values. In the Qur'an, God speaks repeatedly of the essential family unit, the couple, saying:

وَمِن كُلِّ شَيْءٍ خَلَقْنَا زَوْجَيْنِ لَعَلَّكُمْ تَذَكَّرُونَ

And all things We have created by pairs, that haply you may reflect.[7]

The Qur'an describes humankind as originating from a single soul, from which God created every human being, both male and female:

خَلَقَكُم مِّن نَّفْسٍ وَاحِدَةٍ ثُمَّ جَعَلَ مِنْهَا زَوْجَهَا

He created you from one being, then from that (being) He made its mate;[8]

And:

يَا أَيُّهَا النَّاسُ اتَّقُوا رَبَّكُمُ الَّذِي خَلَقَكُم مِّن نَّفْسٍ وَاحِدَةٍ وَخَلَقَ مِنْهَا زَوْجَهَا وَبَثَّ
مِنْهُمَا رِجَالاً كَثِيرًا وَنِسَاء وَاتَّقُوا اللّهَ الَّذِي تَسَاءلُونَ بِهِ وَالأَرْحَامَ إِنَّ اللّهَ كَانَ
عَلَيْكُمْ رَقِيبًا

---

[7] Sūratu 'dh-Dhāriyāt (The Scatterers), 51:49.
[8] Sūratu 'z-Zumar (The Companies), 39:6.

O mankind! Be careful of your duty to your Lord, Who created you from a single soul and from it created its mate and from them twain spread abroad a multitude of men and women. Be careful of your duty toward Allah, in Whom you claim (your rights) of one another, and toward the wombs (that bear you). Lo! Allah has been a watcher over you.[9]

Since God created both male and female from a single, primordial soul, the married couple must share the quintessential qualities of humankind: compassion, mercy, tenderness, dignity and honor, as described in another verse:

وَمِنْ آيَاتِهِ أَنْ خَلَقَ لَكُم مِّنْ أَنفُسِكُمْ أَزْوَاجًا لِّتَسْكُنُوا إِلَيْهَا وَجَعَلَ بَيْنَكُم مَّوَدَّةً وَرَحْمَةً إِنَّ فِي ذَٰلِكَ لَآيَاتٍ لِّقَوْمٍ يَتَفَكَّرُونَ

And among His Signs is this: He created for you mates from among yourselves, that you may dwell in tranquility with them, and He has put love and mercy between your (hearts). Verily, in that are Signs for those who reflect. [10]

Here God describes husband and wife as "dwelling" in one another. The Arabic term used is *taskunū*. It is derived from the word for tranquility, which implies that the husband is a home and place of tranquility for the wife, as the wife is for the husband. Thus, God shows that both husband and wife have equal rights and responsibilities, especially in behavior, towards one another. In other words, a just and fair balance must be set in order to maintain a tranquil, happy home. Love, mercy and reverence are the measure of a marriage.

The Qur'an also says of the marital relationship:

هُنَّ لِبَاسٌ لَّكُمْ وَأَنتُمْ لِبَاسٌ لَّهُنَّ

They are raiment for you and you are raiment for them.[11]

---

[9] Sūratu 'n-Nisā' (Women), 4:1.
[10] Sūrah Rūm (The Romans), 30:21.
[11] Sūratu 'l-Baqarah (The Cow), 2:187.

A garment provides protection, hides faults, maintains dignity and beautifies the wearer. This is what husband and wife do for each other according to the Qur'anic ideal of conjugal relations. The balanced wording of the verse also demonstrates women's rights as equal with men. In this way, the Qur'an establishes the structure of the marital relationship by putting each individual on an equal footing. As they share one original soul, it only follows that they must dwell together in tranquility, love and mercy. A true family institution can only exist when each side complements and completes the other, just as a lamp without electricity will not give light any more than will electricity without a lamp. The two halves, male and female, need each other. Thus, God describes spouses as garments for one another.

> In Islam, both husband and wife have equal rights and responsibilities. Therefore, a fair balance must be set to maintain a tranquil, happy home.

In the first verse of the chapter titled "Women," God also calls on Muslims to "reverence the wombs (that bore you)"[12] —an abstract of Islam's teachings regarding the treatment of women. Treating women harmfully is forbidden in the Holy Qur'an:

وَلَا تُمْسِكُوهُنَّ ضِرَارًا لِتَعْتَدُوا

Retain them (your wives) not to their hurt so that you transgress (the limits).[13]

وَعَاشِرُوهُنَّ بِالْمَعْرُوفِ

But consort with them (your wives) in kindness.[14]

---

[12] Sūratu 'n-Nisā' (Women), 4:34, A. Yusuf Ali, The Holy Qur'an.
[13] Sūratu 'l-Baqarah (The Cow), 2:231.
[14] Sūratu 'n-Nisā' (Women), 4:19.

If we review the breadth of scholarship on the subject, we find that even hard-line Islamists like Syed Qutb have written:

> *Let us go over what we have clarified earlier in terms of the honor which Allah bestowed on both aspects (male and female) of the human being; and in terms of women's rights which stems from her human character; and in terms of the Muslim woman retaining her civic personality along with all the rights which come with it...the right to choose her partner in life, the right to manage her own affairs and the right to manage her own money...*
>
> *It is in no way a battle between men and women. These methods are not meant to crush the head of a woman who starts to deviate, in order to put her back in chains like you would do with a wild dog. This is absolutely not Islam. These are cultural practices which pertain to certain regions and which took place during certain ages when not just one aspect of the human being was degraded, but the whole human being became morally degraded ... (under the control of lust).*[15]

As we further examine the Qur'anic verse which some of today's more conservative literalist commentators cite to sanction wife-beating, we must keep in mind what the Prophet (s) said about the purpose of Islam:

قال النبي صلى الله عليه وسلم"انما بعثت لأتمم مكارم الأخلا

I have been sent to perfect the moral character of people.[16]

For this reason, God said:

وَلاَ تَنسَوُاْ الْفَضْلَ بَيْنَكُمْ

And forget not kindness among yourselves (men and women).[17]

---

[15] Syed Qutb, Fī Dhilāl al-Qur'ān (In the Shades of the Qur'ān), Volume 2 (Cairo: Dār ash-shurūq, 2005), pp. 650-653.

[16] Imam Bukhārī, Adab al-mufrad, no. 372, as cited in Kanz al-‹Ummāl, No. 7125, from al-Maktabat al-Islamī website, retrieved August 30, 2010 from http://www.al-eman.com/Islamlib/viewchp.asp?BID=137&CID=86.

[17] Sūratu 'l-Baqarah (The Cow), 2:237.

بألمعروفِ عليْهنّ ألذى مثلُ لهنّ و

They (women) have rights similar to those (of men)
over them in kindness.[18]

Even when married life has become unbearable, the Qur'an states that the spouses must go their separate ways in peace:

وَإن امْرَأةٌ خَافَتْ مِن بَعْلِهَا نُشُوزًا أوْ إعْرَاضًا فَلاَ جُنَاحَ عَلَيْهمَا أن يُصلِحَا
بَيْنَهُمَا صُلحًا وَالصُّلحُ خَيْرٌ

If a woman fears ill treatment from her husband, or desertion,
it is no sin for them twain if they make terms of peace
between themselves. Peace is better than separating.[19]

Note here the reference to "ill treatment ... from her husband." In this verse, God makes cruelty grounds for a wife to seek divorce with no qualifications.[20] Where then, in a family and community structure that upholds human dignity, is there place for the sanctioned cruelty, violence and anger which wife-beating entails?

ꕤ ꕤ

---

[18] Sūratu 'l-Baqarah (The Cow), 2:228.

[19] Sūratu 'n-Nisā' (Women), 4:128.

[20] According to the *khul‘* method of divorce, the woman is granted a divorce upon agreeing to give up her dowry, a sum obligated on the husband, agreed upon at the time of the marriage.

A Linguistic Exploration of the Word "*Ḍaraba*"

Interpreting the Qur'an through the Qur'an

Now that we have discussed the socio-historical context of the verse, and placed it in the broader context of Qur'anic humanism, we can embark upon a linguistic exploration of the contentious word *ḍaraba*. Classical commentators believe the best understanding of Qur'anic terminology comes from the Holy Qur'an itself, seeking the meaning of a word in one verse by studying its use in other verses. In the case of the root word *ḍaraba*, one finds this verb used fifty-eight times in the Qur'an, in various forms, each with its own meaning and context. While typically translated as "beat," this word also has many other meanings.

For example, the same verb can be translated as "to tap," "to mix," "to mingle," "to separate," "to oscillate," "to fly," "to incline towards," "to throb," "to multiply," "to play music," "to move," "to go for a walk," "to migrate," "to settle down," "to dwell," and "to quote a wise saying," among others (see Appendix). In fact, the root word *ḍaraba* has over fifty derivations and meanings in even the most abridged Arabic dictionary (Hans-Wehr).[21]

In many cases, the verb *ḍaraba* is modified by another word, usually a noun or preposition, relating to the object of the verb; for example, "to range about," "to strike one's notice," "to take an active part," "to impart wisdom," "to pitch a tent," etc. The modifier has an impact on the meaning. However, in the case of the verse in question, there is no modifier in the original Arabic. In only one other instance in the Qur'an is *ḍaraba* used without such a modifier. <u>In such unusual cases, the modifier is often inferred.</u> Thus, the door is left open to a multitude of jurisprudentially legitimate and linguistically valid meanings.

Let us examine some of the possible meanings of the word *ḍaraba* in the Qur'anic text. There are fifty-eight different uses of the verb *ḍaraba* with different meanings or shades of meaning (see Appendix).

---

[21] 1909-1981; a German Arabist.

> The best understanding of Qur'anic terminology comes from the Holy Qur'an itself, seeking the meaning of a word in one verse by studying its use in other verses. The root word "*ḍaraba*" has over fifty derivations.

All of these uses of *ḍaraba* can be interpolated into verse 4:34, and each yields a meaning different from "beat."

The inference of words and meanings into verses of the Qur'an is a common practice in Qur'anic interpretation, one followed by the classical commentators of the first generation until today. In fact, nearly all scholars commonly infer words into this verse: for example, "As to those women ... admonish them (first), (Next), refuse to share their beds, (And last) beat them (lightly)."[22]

Here, each of the words in parentheses is inferred. They do not exist in the Arabic text. In doing this, scholars invoke the need for linguistic and semantic accuracy, as well as reasonableness. All of this is due to the extremely concise wording of the Qur'an. That is why the Qur'an must not always be taken literally, but must be interpreted linguistically, juristically and culturally. If this is not done, the verse reads: "admonish them, separate from them in bed, and beat them (lightly)," eliminating the stages of rectification, and rather applying them all at once. This interpretation would contradict the Qur'anic tradition of moderation in all affairs, and as a result is rarely supported by scholars.

[22] Sūratu 'n-Nisā' (Women), 4:34, A. Yusuf Ali, *The Holy Qur'an.*

Ten Qur'anic Meanings of "*Ḍaraba*"

The most common use of this word in the Holy Qur'an is not with the meaning "to beat," but as verb phrases that provide us with a variety of different meanings:

1. "To hold up as an example," as in, وَلَمَّا ضُرِبَ ابْنُ مَرْيَمَ مَثَلاً *Wa lamma ḍuriba ibnu maryama mathalan,* "When (Jesus) the son of Mary is held up as an example…" [23]

2. "To coin the similitude" as in, إِنَّ أللهَ لا يسْتَحْىِء أن يَضْرِبَ مَثَلاً مَّا بَعُوضَةً *in allaha la yastaḥyi an yaḍriba mathalan mā ba'ūḍatan,* "Lo! Allah disdains not to coin the similitude even of a gnat."[24]

   Similarly, in variant linguistic forms:

3. "To coin," as in, كذلك يَضْرِبُ اللهُ الحَقَّ وَالْبَاطِلَ *kadhālika yaḍribu Allāhu al-ḥaqqa wa al-bāṭila,*"Thus Allah coins (the similitude of) the true and the false."[25]

4. "To cite an example of bad behavior" as in, ضَرَبَ اللَّهُ مَثَلًا لِّلَّذِينَ كَفَرُوا امْرَأَةَ نُوحٍ وَامْرَأَةَ لُوطٍ كَانَتَا تَحْتَ عَبْدَيْنِ مِنْ عِبَادِنَا صَالِحَيْنِ فَخَانَتَاهُمَا فَلَمْ يُغْنِيَا عَنْهُمَا مِنَ اللَّهِ شَيْئًا *ḍaraba allahu mathalan lilladhīna kafarū amrāta nuḥin w'amrāta lūṭin kānata taḥta 'abdayni min 'ibādina ṣāliḥayni fakhānatāhumā falam yughniyā 'anhumā min allahi shay'an,* "Allah cites an example for those who disbelieve: the wife of Noah and the wife of Lot, who were under two of Our righteous slaves, yet betrayed them so that they (the husbands) availed them naught against Allah."[26]

If we reexamine the verse in question in light of these references, it should yield a meaning closer to, "Separate from them in bed, (and) cite an example to them (or coin a similitude for them)," which could mean, "make a comparison of their behavior to those who were chastised in the Qur'an," (*e.g.*, the wives of Noah and Lot).

---

[23] Sūratu z-Zukhruf (The Embellishment), 43:57.

[24] Sūratu 'l-Baqarah (The Cow), 2:26.

[25] Sūratu 'r-Ra'd (The Thunder), 13:17.

[26] Sūratu't-Taḥrīm (The Prohibition), 66:10.

Other uses of *ḍaraba* in the Qur'an that do not have the meaning "to strike" or "to beat" are:

5. "To brand with or to stamp upon," as in, وَضُرِبَتْ عَلَيْهِمُ الذِّلَّةُ وَالْمَسْكَنَةُ *wa ḍuribat 'alayhim adh-dhillatu wal-maskana,* "And humiliation and wretchedness were stamped upon them."[27]

In this sense the verse would read, "Separate from them in bed, (and) brand them with their wrongdoing," in the sense of, "make it known widely that they are misbehaving," or, "separate from them in bed, (and) brand them with humiliation;" that is, "make known their ill conduct so they will be shamed into abstaining from it."

6. "To strike a path," as in فَاضْرِبْ لَهُمْ طَرِيقًا فِي الْبَحْرِ *faḍrib lahum ṭarīqan fi'l-baḥri,* "And strike for them a dry path in the sea."[28]

In this sense the verse would read, "Separate from them in bed, (and) strike a path for them," meaning, "Show them a path to self-examination and self-correction," or, "Show them a path to leave, a way out," meaning the relationship has come to an end.

7. "To go about," as in, إِذَا ضَرَبُوا فِي الأَرْضِ *idhā ḍarabū fi'l-arḍi,* "Who went abroad in the land."[29]

In this sense the verse would read, "Separate from them in bed, (and) leave them." This meaning was recently given a great deal of press after Dr. Laleh Bakhtiar preferred it in her translation of the Qur'an.

8. "To set forth," as in, مَا ضَرَبُوهُ لَكَ إِلاَّ جَدَلاً *mā ḍarabūhu laka illa jadalan,* "This they set forth to you, only by way of disputation."[30]

---

[27] Sūratu 'l-Baqarah (The Cow), 2:61.
[28] Sūrah ṬāḤā, 20:77.
[29] Sūrat Āli-'Imrān (The Family of Imrān), 3:156.
[30] Sūratu z-Zukhruf (The Embellishments), 43:58.

In this sense, the verse would read, "Separate from them in bed, (and) set forth to them;" that is, "expound to them their wrongdoing."

9. "To set up," as in, فَضُرِبَ بَيْنَهُم بِسُورٍ- *faḍuriba baynahum bi-sūrin*, "Then there will separate them a wall."[31]

In this sense the verse would read, "Separate from them in bed, (and) set up a barrier (between you and them)."

10. "To draw over," as in, وَلْيَضْرِبْنَ بِخُمُرِهِنَّ عَلَى جُيُوبِهِنَّ *wal-yaḍribna bi-khumūrihinna 'ala juyūbihinna*, "and to draw their veils over their bosoms."[32]

In this sense the verse would read, "Separate from them in bed, (and) then lovingly draw them towards you," meaning, after the pressure of separation the warmth of affection will restart the relationship afresh.

The last verse compared is particularly important, because it applies specifically to women. Given the absence of debate over how *ḍaraba* is interpreted in this particular context, why should it carry such a different meaning in the verse in question?

Other Interpretations

There are other meanings of the word *ḍaraba* that are not used in the Holy Qur'an. The Arabic-English Dictionary, *al-Mawrid*[33] gives over thirty different meanings for *ḍaraba*. The *Hans-Wehr Arabic-English Dictionary*[34] lists over fifty. Let us examine how some of these different translations may apply to the verse in question.

---

[31] Sūratu 'l-Ḥadīd (The Iron), 57:13.

[32] Sūratu 'n-Nūr (The Light), 24:31.

[33] Rūḥī al-Ba'albakī, Al-Mawrid: *A Modern Arabic-English Dictionary* (15th edition) (Dār al-'Ilm li'l-Malāyīn, 2001), p. 706.

[34] *Hans-Wehr Arabic-English Dictionary of Modern Written Arabic,* ed. J.M. Cowan (Spoken Language Services, Ithaca, 1976), pp. 538-540.

One pertinent dictionary meaning of the verb *ḍaraba* is, "to have sexual intercourse." In other languages as well, the verb 'to strike' is also used to mean engagement in sexual intercourse: for example, Somali, a derivate language of Arabic, uses the verb with this meaning. Even the old Germanic verb *focken*, "to strike," became a well-known vulgarism for sexual intercourse in English.

One of the great early classical commentators on the Qur'an, al-Zamakhsharī, stated:

> *It is said that it (ḍaraba) means, 'have intercourse with them and then hold them firmly...,' and this is the meaning given by the greatest commentators (of the Holy Quran).*[35]

In his classical commentary on the Qur'an, *al-Mufradāt fi gharīb al-Qur'ān*, Rāghib al-Asfahānī gives the meanings of these words with special reference to this verse, noting that *ḍaraba* metaphorically means "to have sexual relations." In this one case, the verb *ḍaraba* stands alone with no object, as Rāghib cites, وضَرَبَ الفحلُ الناقة *ḍaraba al-faḥl an-nāqah,* "The stallion camel covered the mare camel,"[36] which appears in the same linguistic form as the verse under consideration. This is cited as well in the foremost Arabic dictionary, al-Ifrīqī's *Lisān al-'Arab.*[37]

The great Sufi scholar al-Qushayrī said in his commentary on the verse in his *Laṭā'if al-ishārāt bi tafsīr al-Qur'ān*:

أي ارتقوا في تهذيبهن بالتدريج والرفق، وإنْ صَلَحَ الأمر بالوعظ فلا تستعمل العصا بالضرب، فالآية تتضمن آداب العِشْرة.

What is meant here is to encourage them to correct themselves in stages and with kindness. But if the matter is settled by

---

35 Abū al-Qāsim Maḥmūd ibn ‹Umar al-Zamakhsharī, *Al-Kashshāf ‹an Haqā'iq at-Tanzil (*Egypt: Dār al-Kutub al-'Ilmīyyah, 2003) retrieved August 30,2010, from altafsir website: http://www.altafsir.com/Tafasir.asp?tMadhNo=1&tTafsirNo=2&tSoraNo=4&tAyahNo=34&tDisplay=yes&Page=2&Size=1&LanguageId=1:
وقيل: معناه أكرهوهن على الجماع واربطوهن، من هجر البعير إذا شدّه بالهجار. وهذا من تفسير الثقلاء

36 Rāghib al-Asfahānī, *al-Mufradāt fi gharīb al-Qur'ān* (Beirut: Dār al-Ma'rifah, 1999), retrieved August 30, 2010, from altafsir website: http://www.altafsir.com/MiscellaneousBooks.asp, Section letter *ḍād*, word: *ḍarab.*

37 Ibn Mundhir al-Ifrīqī, *Lisān al-'Arab* (Egypt: al-Maṭba'at al-Kubra al-Mīrīah, 1979), section letter *ḍād*, 33.

> admonishing then one should not beat her (with a stick or the hand) because the verse implies the conduct of engaging in sexual relations.[38]

This interpretation fits the context of the verse exceedingly well. The *ḍaraba* stage in the process follows temporary suspension of relations between the spouses. Note also that among the many meanings of this term, "to mingle" is used here in opposition to the sense of separation contained in the verb *uḥjur*, which means "to separate from them in bed," immediately preceding, while "inclining towards," "mingling," "settling down," and "having sexual intercourse" are looking ahead to the marital reconciliation (*tawfīq*) in the next phrase (*w 'aḍribūhunna*). This is a good example of the subtle and intricate ways in which meanings interlace in the Holy Qur'an, an aspect often lost in translation.

We also know from other statements of the Prophet (s) that God showers a couple with spiritual blessings when they engage in licit sexual relations. In this context, then, the verse can be translated:

> *As for women on whose part you fear disloyalty and ill conduct, (first) admonish them; (next), separate from them in bed; (and last) go to bed with them (when they are willing).*

Another linguistic meaning we find is, "to turn away," "to disregard," and, "to avoid speaking," in each case with the qualifier that one should look to intermediaries to solve the issue. This coincides with the verse which follows, saying:

وَإِنْ خِفْتُمْ شِقَاقَ
بَيْنِهِمَا فَابْعَثُوا حَكَماً مِّنْ أَهْلِهِ وَحَكَماً مِّنْ أَهْلِهَا..

> *And if you fear a breach between them twain (the man and wife), appoint an arbiter from his folk and an arbiter from her folk.*[39]

---

[38] Abū 'l-Qāsim 'Abdu 'l-Karīm al-Qushayrī, *Laṭā'if al-isharat bi tafsīr al-Qur'ān* (Egypt: Dār al-Kutub al-'Ilmīyyah, 2000), retrieved August 30, 2010 from altafsir website: http://www.altafsir.com/Tafasir.asp?tMadhNo=0&tTafsirNo=31&tSoraNo=4&tAyahNo=34&tDisplay=yes&UserProfile=0&LanguageId=1.

[39] Sūratu 'n-Nisā' (Women), 4:35

> Imam Suyuti reasoned that a wife should not be beaten, but rather softness and good conduct should be shown her and, if necessary, outside parties should intervene to restore marital accord.

The renowned Qur'anic commentator, Imām as-Sūyūṭi (d. 911, Egypt), says in his *Durar*:

> *If strife ensues between a man and wife, he should seek counsel from the righteous men and someone who is his peer in righteousness among the women so they can determine which one of the two is in the wrong (and help them correct it).*[40]

In this context, beating would not be used, but rather softness, good conduct, and the intervention of outside parties.

[40] Jalāl al-dīn as-Suyūṭī, *Al-durar al-manthūr fī tafsīr bi'l ma'thūr*, retrieved August 30, 2010 from altafsir website: http://www.altafsir.com/Tafasir.asp?tMadhNo=0&tTafsirNo=26&tSoraNo=4&tAyahNo=35&tDisplay=yes&UserProfile=0&LanguageId=1.

The Importance of Prophet Muhammad's Example

Finally, in our exploration of verse 4:34, it is imperative that we also look to the behavior of the Prophet Muhammad (s) for our example, for God said:

مَّنْ يُطِعِ الرَّسُولَ فَقَدْ أَطَاعَ اللَّهَ

Whoso obeys the messenger has obeyed Allah.[41]

God also said:

قُلْ إِن كُنتُمْ تُحِبُّونَ اللَّهَ فَاتَّبِعُونِي يُحْبِبْكُمُ اللَّهُ وَيَغْفِرْ لَكُمْ
ذُنُوبَكُمْ وَاللَّهُ غَفُورٌ رَّحِيمٌ

Say, (O Muhammad, to mankind), "If you love Allah, follow me;
Allah will love you and forgive you your sins.
Allah is Forgiving, Merciful."[42]

Accordingly, following the example of the Prophet (s) is a must for all faithful Muslims. When we take into account the Prophet's (s) teachings of kindness to women, including the many statements (*ḥadīth*) in which he specifically prohibited wife-beating, we must conclude that *ḍaraba* cannot possibly mean striking to violently hurt another.

Prophet Muhammad's High Regard for Women

It is reported that, just after the revelation of the verse in question, when some of his companions took the word *"w 'aḍribūhunna"* literally, and struck their wives, the Prophet (s) objected to their behavior, saying:

فقال النبي صلى الله عليه وسلم: "لقد طاف بآل محمد نساءٌ كثيرٌ يشكون
أزواجهنَّ، ليس أولئك بخياركم

Indeed, a large group of women gathered here, in my house, complaining about their husbands. You will not find those men the best of you.

---

[41] Sūratu 'n-Nisā' (Women), 4:80.

[42] Sūrat Āli-'Imrān (The Family of Imrān), 3:31.

Rather, the Prophet (s) instructed his Companions:

قال: "أطعموهنَّ مما تأكلون، واكسوهنَّ مما تكتسون، ولا تضربوهن، ولا تُقبِّحُوهُن

Give them food from what you eat, clothe them as you clothe yourself and do not beat them, and do not revile them.[43]

قال (النبي)" ألا وَاسْتَوْصُوا بالنساء خيراً فإنهن عَوَانٍ عندكم .. ألا إنّ لكم على نسائكم حقّاً ولنسائكم عليكم حقّاً فأما ..."

I remind you concerning women to do good! They are your committed helpers and companions.... Indeed you have on your women rights and your women have rights on you....[44]

This is in concert with the ethos of Islam as a faith, where the Prophet (s) said:

قالَ رَسُولُ اللَّهِ صلى الله عليه وسلم "لَا ضَرَرَ وَلَا ضِرَارَ"

There is no harm and no retribution (in religion).[45]

And in another version, God's Messenger (s) said:

فَاتَّقُوا اللَّهَ عَزَّ وَجَلَّ فِي النِّسَاءِ فَإِنَّهُنَّ عِنْدَكُمْ عَوَانٌ لَا يَمْلِكْنَ لِأَنْفُسِهِنَّ شَيْئًا وَإِنَّ لَهُنَّ عَلَيْكُمْ وَلَكُمْ عَلَيْهِنَّ حَقًّا ...

Fear Allah, the Exalted, in respect to your women! For verily they are your committed partners and helpers, they hold nothing for themselves, and indeed they have rights on you and you have rights on them ... "

Finally, the Prophet (s) said:

---

[43] Sulaymān ibn Ash'ath Abū Dāwūd as-Sijistānī al-Azdī, *Sunan Abū Dāwūd* (Beirut: Dār al-Fikr), No. 2144.

44 Imām Tirmidhī, *Sunan at-Tirmidhī* (Beirut: Dār Iḥyā' al-Turath al-'Arabī, n.d), No. 1851.

[45] Ibn Mājah al-Qazwīnī, *Sunan Ibn Mājah*, ed. Maḥmūd Fu'ād 'Abd al-Bāqī (Beirut: Dār al-Fikr, n.d) Kitāb al-Aḥkām, Nos. 2430, 2431; Mālik ibn Anas Abū 'Abdullāh al-Asbāḥī, *Muwaṭṭa Imām Mālik*, Section of Offices (Damascus: Dār al-Qalam, 1991).

قال رسول الله صلى الله عليه وسلم:- "خيركم خيركم لأهله، وأنا خيركم لأهلي

The best of you is the best to his family
and I am the best among you to my family.[46]

Prophet Muhammad (s) explicitly forbade the beating of any woman, saying:

خرج عبد الرزاق وابن سعد وابن المنذر والحاكم والبيهقي عن إياس بن عبد الله ابن أبي ذئاب قال: قال رسول الله صلى الله عليه وسلم:
"لا تضربوا إماء الله"

Never beat the handmaidens of God.[47]

The Prophet (s) also said:

إذا استنشقت فبالغ إلا أن تكون صائما ولا تضرب ظعينتك كما تضرب أمتك

Do not beat your noble wife like a slave.[48]

Also:

وأخرج عبد الرزاق عن عائشة عن النبي صلى الله عليه وسلم قال:
أما يستحي أحدكم أن يضرب امرأته كما يضرب العبد، يضربها
أول النهارثمّ يضاجعها آخره

Are you not ashamed to beat your wives as one beats a slave; you beat her in the daytime and have intercourse with her in the night?[49]

Speaking more generally, the Prophet (s) said:

أخبرنا أبو نصر بن قتادة أنا أبو علي الرفاء القروي أنا علي بن عبد العزيز ثنا أبو غسان مالك بن إسماعيل ثنا اسرائيل عن الأعمش عن شقيق عن عبد الله قال قال رسول الله صلى الله عليه وسلم اجيبوا الداعي ولا تردوا الهدية ولا تضربوا الناس أو المسلمين

Respond when someone calls you, do not refuse a gift,
and beat neither the people nor the Muslims.[50]

---

[46] Muhammad ibn 'Īsā al-Tirmidhī, *Sunan at-Tirmidhī* (Beirut: Dār Iḥyā' al-Turāth al-'Arabī, n.d.), No. 3985.

[47] Abū Dāwūd as-Sijistānī, *Sunan Abū Dāwūd*, No. 2144.

48 al-Nisābūrī, *Al-Mustadrak 'alā as-saḥīḥayn*, Vol. 1 (Beirut: Dār al-ma'rifah, 1998), No. 524

[49] 'Abd ar-Razzāq as-San'ānī, *Mūsānnaf 'Abd ar-Razzāq*, Vol. 9 (Beirut: Al-Maktab al-Islāmī, 1982-3), p. 442.

> Prophet Muhammad's teachings of kindness to women and the many *aḥadīth* in which he prohibited wife-beating demonstrate that "*ḍaraba*" cannot possibly mean "strike to violently hurt another."

The following *aḥādīth* are also related:

وعن أبي أمامة أن رسول الله صلى الله عليه وسلم وهب لعلي غلاما فقال لا تضربه فإني نهيت عن ضرب أهل الصلاة وقد رأيته يصلي

The Prophet (s) sent 'Alī a man servant and said, "Do not beat him, for indeed I have been prohibited from beating those who pray, and I have observed him praying."[51]

وفي المجتبى للدارقطني أن عمر بن الخطاب رضي الله عنه قال نهانا رسول الله صلى الله عليه وسلم عن ضرب المصلين .

'Umar ibn al-Khaṭṭāb related, "The Messenger of Allah (s) prohibited us from beating any Muslim who observes prayers."[52]

Finally, the Prophet Muhammad's (s) wife 'Ā'ishā said:

ما ضرب رسول الله صلى الله عليه وسلم امرأة له ولا خادما قط

The Prophet (s) never beat any of his wives or servants.[53]

---

[50] Aḥmad ibn al-Ḥusayn 'Ali ibn Mūsā Abū Bakr al-Bayhaqī, *Shu'ab al-Imān* (Beirut: Dār al-Kutub al-'Ilmīyyah, 1996), No. 5359 and a similar narration in Aḥmad ibn Ḥanbal, *Al-Musnad* (20 vols.), ed. Aḥmad Shākir and Hamza Aḥmad al-Zayn (Cairo: Dār al-Ḥadīth, 1995), No. 3838 without reference to "the people."

[51] Aḥmad ibn Ḥanbal, *Al-Musnad* (20 vols.), ed. Aḥmad Shākir and Hamza Aḥmad al-Zayn (Cairo: Dār al-ḥadīth, 1995), No. 22208.

[52] 'Alī b. 'Umar al-Dāraqutnī, *al-Sunan* (4 vols.), ed. Shams al-Ḥaqq 'Azīmabādī (Cairo n.d.), No. 1778.

[53] Muhammad Nāṣir al-dīn al-Albānī, *Ghāyat al-Marām fī takhrīj aḥadīth al-ḥalāl wa'l-ḥarām*, 3rd Edition (Beirut: Maktab al-Islami, 1984/1985), No. 252.

Such clear statements by the Prophet (s) are prohibitions for all Muslims, as every believer must strive to follow the Prophet (s) in his or her daily actions. God's Messenger (s) never allowed himself or anyone in his community to raise a hand against another in their family. In light of this, there is no excuse for men to beat their wives and then seek religious means to justify their heinous wrongdoing. Laws that fail to prevent this kind of behavior must be amended.

Conclusion

In a time when political and communal tensions remain high, it is essential that ethical issues such as these should not become a source of friction between communities. It is imperative that each community in our global society seek to understand the other, not through the eyes of extremist scholars, but through the knowledge, understanding and wisdom of broad-minded scholars whose attitude is one of conciliation, not fanaticism.

Islam was revealed as a religion for all times and all conditions. It is the responsibility of our scholars to use their knowledge, experience, and credibility within the community to interpret the faith in a way that upholds the justice, equity, and mercy that God and Prophet Muhammad (s) intended. With that vision and purpose in mind, we unequivocally state that there can be no Islamic grounds for beating one's wife and no religious sanction for spousal abuse. It is now the responsibility of our community leaders to educate their communities accordingly.

Appendix:
Verses That Use the Verb "*Ḍaraba*"

أَلَمْ تَرَ كَيْفَ ضَرَبَ اللَّهُ مَثَلاً كَلِمَةً طَيِّبَةً كَشَجَرةٍ طَيِّبَةٍ

Seest thou not how Allah sets forth a parable?
A goodly word like a goodly tree. (14:24)

ضَرَبَ اللَّهُ مَثَلاً عَبْدًا مَّمْلُوكًا لاَّ يَقْدِرُ عَلَى
شَيْءٍ وَمَن رَّزَقْنَاهُ مِنَّا رِزْقًا حَسَنًا

Allah sets forth the parable (of two men: one) a slave under the dominion of another; He has no power of any sort; and (the other) a man on whom We have bestowed goodly favors from Ourselves. (16:75)

وَضَرَبَ اللَّهُ مَثَلاً رَّجُلَيْنِ

Allah sets forth (another) parable of two men. (16:76)

وَضَرَبَ اللَّهُ مَثَلاً قَرْيَةً كَانَتْ آمِنَةً مُّطْمَئِنَّةً يَأْتِيهَا رِزْقُهَا
رَغَدًا مِّن كُلِّ مَكَانٍ

And Allah sets forth a parable: a city enjoying security and quiet, abundantly supplied with sustenance from every place. (16:112)

ضَرَبَ لَكُم مَّثَلًا مِنْ أَنفُسِكُمْ

He propounds to you a similitude from your own (experience). (30:28)

وَضَرَبَ لَنَا مَثَلًا وَنَسِيَ خَلْقَهُ

And he makes comparisons for Us, and forgets His own (origin and) Creation. (36:78)

ضَرَبَ اللَّهُ مَثَلًا رَّجُلًا فِيهِ شُرَكَاء مُتَشَاكِسُون وَرَجُلًا سَلَمًا لِّرَجُلٍ
هَلْ يَسْتَوِيَانِ مَثَلًا

Allah puts forth a parable: a man belonging to many partners at variance with each other, and a man belonging entirely to one master: are those two equal in comparison? (39:29)

وَإِذَا بُشِّرَ أَحَدُهُم بِمَا ضَرَبَ لِلرَّحْمَنِ مَثَلًا ظَلَّ وَجْهُهُ مُسْوَدًّا وَهُوَ كَظِيمٌ

When news is brought to one of them of (the birth of) what he sets up as a likeness to (Allah) Most Gracious, his face darkens, and he is filled with inward grief! (43:17)

ضَرَبَ اللَّهُ مَثَلًا لِّلَّذِينَ كَفَرُوا اِمْرَأَةَ نُوح
وَاِمْرَأَةَ لُوطٍ كَانَتَا تَحْتَ عَبْدَيْنِ مِنْ عِبَادِنَا صَالِحَيْنِ

Allah sets forth, for an example to the unbelievers, the wife of Noah and the wife of Lut: they were (respectively) under two of our righteous servants. (66:10)

وَضَرَبَ اللَّهُ مَثَلًا لِّلَّذِينَ آمَنُوا اِمْرَأَةَ فِرْعَوْنَ

And Allah sets forth, as an example to those who believe, the wife of Pharaoh. (66:11)

يَا أَيُّهَا الَّذِينَ آمَنُوا إِذَا ضَرَبْتُمْ فِي سَبِيلِ اللَّهِ فَتَبَيَّنُوا

O you who believe! When you go abroad in the cause of Allah, investigate carefully. (4:94)

وَإِذَا ضَرَبْتُمْ فِي الأَرْضِ فَلَيْسَ عَلَيْكُمْ جُنَاحٌ أَن تَقْصُرُوا مِنَ الصَّلاَةِ

When you travel through the earth, there is no blame on you if you shorten your prayers. (4:101)

إِنْ أَنتُمْ ضَرَبْتُمْ فِي الأَرْضِ فَأَصَابَتْكُم مُّصِيبَةُ المَوْتِ

If you are journeying through the earth,
and the chance of death befalls you. (5:106)

وَضَرَبْنَا لَكُمُ الأَمْثَالَ

And We put forth (many) parables in your behoof! (14:45)

فَضَرَبْنَا عَلَى آذَانِهِمْ فِي الْكَهْفِ سِنِينَ عَدَدًا

Then We draw (a veil) over their ears,
for a number of years, in the cave. (18:11)

وَكُلًّا ضَرَبْنَا لَهُ الْأَمْثَالَ

To each one We set forth parables and examples. (25:39)

وَلَقَدْ ضَرَبْنَا لِلنَّاسِ فِي هَذَا الْقُرْآنِ مِن كُلِّ مَثَلٍ

Verily, We have propounded for men in this Qur'an
every kind of parable. (30:58)

وَلَقَدْ ضَرَبْنَا لِلنَّاسِ فِي هَذَا الْقُرْآنِ مِن كُلِّ مَثَلٍ لَّعَلَّهُمْ يَتَذَكَّرُونَ

We have put forth for men in this Qur'an every kind of parable,
in order that they may receive admonition. (39:27)

وَقَالُواْ لِإِخْوَانِهِمْ إِذَا ضَرَبُواْ فِي الأَرْضِ
أَوْ كَانُواْ غُزًّى لَّوْ كَانُواْ عِندَنَا مَا مَاتُواْ وَمَا قُتِلُواْ

Be not like the unbelievers who say of their brethren when they
are travelling through the earth or engaged in fighting, "If they had
stayed with us, they would not have died or been slain." (3:156)

انظُرْ كَيْفَ ضَرَبُواْ لَكَ الأَمْثَالَ فَضَلُّواْ فَلاَ يَسْتَطِيعُونَ سَبِيلاً

See what similes they strike for you, but they have gone astray, and never can they find a way. (17:48)

انظُرْ كَيْفَ ضَرَبُوا لَكَ الْأَمْثَالَ فَضَلُّوا فَلَا يَسْتَطِيعُونَ سَبِيلًا

See what kinds of comparisons they make for you! But they have gone astray, and never a way will they be able to find! (25:9)

وَقَالُوا أَآلِهَتُنَا خَيْرٌ أَمْ هُوَ مَا ضَرَبُوهُ لَكَ إِلَّا جَدَلًا بَلْ هُمْ قَوْمٌ خَصِمُونَ

And they say, "Are our gods best, or He?" This they set forth to you, only by way of disputation: yea, they are a contentious people. (43:58)

فَلاَ تَضْرِبُواْ لِلّهِ الأَمْثَالَ إِنَّ اللّهَ يَعْلَمُ وَأَنتُمْ لاَ تَعْلَمُونَ

Invent not similitudes for Allah, for Allah knows and you know not. (16:74)

أَفَنَضْرِبُ عَنكُمُ الذِّكْرَ صَفْحًا أَن كُنتُمْ قَوْمًا مُّسْرِفِينَ

Shall We then take away the Message from you and repel (you), for that you are a people transgressing beyond bounds? (43:5)

وَتِلْكَ الْأَمْثَالُ نَضْرِبُهَا لِلنَّاسِ وَمَا يَعْقِلُهَا إِلَّا الْعَالِمُونَ

And such are the parables We set forth for mankind, but only those with knowledge understand them. (29:43)

وَتِلْكَ الْأَمْثَالُ نَضْرِبُهَا لِلنَّاسِ لَعَلَّهُمْ يَتَفَكَّرُونَ

Such are the similitudes which We propound to men, that they may reflect. (59:21)

إِنَّ اللَّهَ لاَ يَسْتَحْيِي أَن يَضْرِبَ مَثَلاً مَّا بَعُوضَةً فَمَا فَوْقَهَا

Allah disdains not to use the similitude of things, lowest as well as highest. (2:26)

كَذَلِكَ يَضْرِبُ اللّهُ الْحَقَّ وَالْبَاطِلَ

Thus does Allah (by parables) show forth truth and vanity. (13:17)

كَذَلِكَ يَضْرِبُ اللّهُ الأَمْثَالَ

Thus does Allah set forth parables. (13:17)

وَيَضْرِبُ اللّهُ الأَمْثَالَ لِلنَّاسِ لَعَلَّهُمْ يَتَذَكَّرُونَ

So Allah sets forth parables for men, in order that they may receive admonition. (14:25)

وَيَضْرِبُ اللَّهُ الْأَمْثَالَ لِلنَّاسِ

Allah sets forth parables for men. (24:35)

كَذَلِكَ يَضْرِبُ اللَّهُ لِلنَّاسِ أَمْثَالَهُمْ

Thus does Allah set forth for men their lessons by similitudes. (47:3)

وَلْيَضْرِبْنَ بِخُمُرِهِنَّ عَلَى جُيُوبِهِنَّ

That they should draw their veils over their bosoms. (24:31)

وَلَا يَضْرِبْنَ بِأَرْجُلِهِنَّ لِيُعْلَمَ مَا يُخْفِينَ مِن زِينَتِهِنَّ

And that they should not strike their feet in order to draw attention to their hidden ornaments. (24:31)

الْمَلآئِكَةُ يَضْرِبُونَ وُجُوهَهُمْ وَأَدْبَارَهُم

(How) the angels smite their faces and their backs. (8:50)

فَكَيْفَ إِذَا تَوَفَّتْهُمُ الْمَلَائِكَةُ يَضْرِبُونَ وُجُوهَهُمْ وَأَدْبَارَهُمْ

But how (will it be) when the angels take their souls at death,
and smite their faces and their backs? (47:27)

عَلِمَ أَن سَيَكُونُ مِنكُم مَّرْضَى وَآخَرُونَ يَضْرِبُونَ فِي الْأَرْضِ

He knows that there may be (some) among you in ill health,
others travelling through the land. (73:20)

وَإِذِ اسْتَسْقَى مُوسَى لِقَوْمِهِ فَقُلْنَا اضْرِب بِّعَصَاكَ الْحَجَرَ
فَانفَجَرَتْ مِنْهُ اثْنَتَا عَشْرَةَ عَيْناً

And remember Moses prayed for water for his people. We said, "Strike the rock with your staff." Then gushed forth therefrom twelve springs. (2:60)

وَأَوْحَيْنَا إِلَى مُوسَى إِذِ اسْتَسْقَاهُ قَوْمُهُ أَنِ اضْرِب بِّعَصَاكَ الْحَجَرَ
فَانبَجَسَتْ مِنْهُ اثْنَتَا عَشْرَةَ عَيْنًا

We directed Moses by inspiration, when his (thirsty) people asked
him for water: "Strike the rock with your staff." Out of it
there gushed forth twelve springs. (7:160)

وَاضْرِبْ لَهُم مَّثَلًا رَّجُلَيْنِ

Set forth to them the parable of two men. (18:32)

وَاضْرِبْ لَهُم مَّثَلَ الْحَيَاةِ الدُّنْيَا كَمَاء أَنزَلْنَاهُ مِنَ السَّمَاء

Set forth to them the similitude of the life of this world: it is like
the rain which We send down from the skies. (18:45)

وَلَقَدْ أَوْحَيْنَا إِلَى مُوسَى أَنْ أَسْرِ بِعِبَادِي فَاضْرِبْ لَهُمْ طَرِيقًا فِي الْبَحْرِ يَبَسًا

We sent an inspiration to Moses: "Travel by night with My servants, and strike a dry path for them through the sea. (20:77)

فَأَوْحَيْنَا إِلَى مُوسَى أَنِ اضْرِب بِّعَصَاكَ الْبَحْرَ فَانفَلَقَ فَكَانَ كُلُّ فِرْقٍ كَالطَّوْدِ الْعَظِيمِ

Then We told Moses by inspiration: "Strike the sea with your rod." So it divided, and each separate part became like the huge, firm mass of a mountain. (26:63)

وَاضْرِبْ لَهُم مَّثَلاً أَصْحَابَ الْقَرْيَةِ

Set forth to them, by way of a parable, the (story of) the Companions of the City. (36:13)

وَخُذْ بِيَدِكَ ضِغْثًا فَاضْرِب بِّهِ وَلَا تَحْنَثْ إِنَّا وَجَدْنَاهُ صَابِرًا نِعْمَ الْعَبْدُ إِنَّهُ أَوَّابٌ

(We said:) "And take in your hand a little grass, and strike therewith and break not (your oath)." Truly, We found him full of patience and constancy; how excellent in Our service! Ever did he turn (to Us)! (38:44)

فَاضْرِبُواْ فَوْقَ الأَعْنَاقِ وَاضْرِبُواْ مِنْهُمْ كُلَّ بَنَانٍ

Smite above their necks and smite off all their fingertips! (8:12)

فَقُلْنَا اضْرِبُوهُ بِبَعْضِهَا كَذَلِكَ يُحْيِي اللَّهُ الْمَوْتَى وَيُرِيكُمْ آيَاتِهِ لَعَلَّكُمْ تَعْقِلُونَ

So We said, "Strike the (body) with a piece of the (heifer)." Thus, Allah brings the dead to life and shows you His Signs that you may understand. (2:73)

وَاضْرِبُوهُنَّ فَإِنْ أَطَعْنَكُمْ فَلاَ تَبْغُواْ عَلَيْهِنَّ سَبِيلاً

And (last) beat them (lightly), but if they return to obedience, seek not against them means (of annoyance). (4:34)

يَا أَيُّهَا النَّاسُ ضُرِبَ مَثَلٌ فَاسْتَمِعُوا لَهُ

O men! Here is a parable set forth; listen to it! (22:73)

وَلَمَّا ضُرِبَ ابْنُ مَرْيَمَ مَثَلًا إِذَا قَوْمُكَ مِنْهُ يَصِدُّونَ

When (Jesus) the son of Mary is held up as an example, behold, your people raise a clamor thereat (in ridicule)! (43:57)

فَضُرِبَ بَيْنَهُم بِسُورٍ لَهُ بَابٌ

So a wall will be put up between them, with a gate therein. (57:13)

وَضُرِبَتْ عَلَيْهِمُ الذِّلَّةُ وَالْمَسْكَنَةُ وَبَآؤُوْا بِغَضَبٍ مِّنَ اللَّهِ

They were covered with humiliation and misery; they drew on themselves the wrath of Allah. (2:61)

ضُرِبَتْ عَلَيْهِمُ الذِّلَّةُ أَيْنَ مَا ثُقِفُوا

Shame is pitched over them (like a tent) wherever they are found. (3:112)

وَضُرِبَتْ عَلَيْهِمُ الْمَسْكَنَةُ

And pitched over them is (the tent of) destitution. (3:112)

فَضَرْبَ الرِّقَابِ حَتَّى إِذَا أَثْخَنتُمُوهُمْ فَشُدُّوا الْوَثَاقَ

Smite at their necks; at length, when you have thoroughly subdued them, bind a bond firmly (on them). (47:4)

لِلْفُقَرَاءِ الَّذِينَ أُحصِرُواْ فِي سَبِيلِ اللَّهِ لاَ يَسْتَطِيعُونَ ضَرْبًا فِي الأَرْضِ

(Charity is) for those in need, who in Allah's cause are restricted (from travel) and cannot move about in the land, seeking (trade or work). (2:273)

فَرَاغَ عَلَيْهِمْ ضَرْبًا بِالْيَمِينِ

Then did he turn upon them, striking (them) with the right hand. (37:93)

Glossary of Islamic Terms

adhān: call to prayer.
Alḥamdūlillāh: praise God.
Allāhu Akbar: God is Great.
āyah/āyāt (pl. *Ayāt*): a verse of the Holy Qur'an.
Banī Adam: Children of Adam; humanity.
Bismillāhi'r-Raḥmāni'r-Raḥīm: "In the Name of the All-Merciful, the All-Compassionate"; introductory verse to chapters of the Qur'an.
du'ā: supplication.
dunyā: world; worldly life.
farḍ: obligatory worship.
Fātiḥah: Sūratu 'l-Fātiḥah; the opening chapter of the Qur'an.
ḥadīth Nabawī (pl., *aḥadīth*): prophetic *ḥadīth* whose meaning and linguistic expression are those of Prophet Muhammad.
Hajj: the sacred pilgrimage of Islam obligatory on every mature Muslim once in their life.
ḥalāl: permitted, lawful according to Islamic Sharīʿah.
ḥarām: forbidden, unlawful.
Ḥawā: Eve.
imān: faith, belief.
imām: leader of congregational prayer; an advanced scholar followed by a large community.
jama'ah: group, congregation.
Jannah: Paradise.
Jibrīl : Gabriel, Archangel of revelation.
mahr: dowry, given by the groom to the bride.
Māshā'Allāh: as Allāh Wills.
muʿmin: a believer.
nabī: a prophet of God.
nāfs: lower self, ego.
nūr: light.
raḥmā: mercy.
Ramaḍān: the ninth month of the Islamic calendar; month of fasting.
ṣadaqah: voluntary charity.
ṣaḥīḥ: authentic; term certifying validity of a *ḥadīth* of the Prophet.
ṣalāt: ritual prayer, one of the five obligatory pillars of Islam. Also, to invoke blessing on the Prophet.
salām: peace.
Salām, as-: "The Peaceful"; a divine name. *As-salāmu ʿalaykum:* "Peace be upon you." (Islamic greeting).
subḥānAllāh: glory be to God.
sūnnah: Practices of Prophet Muhammad in actions and words; what he did, said, recommended, or approved of in his Companions.
sūrah: a chapter of the Qur'an; picture, image.
tafsīr: to explain, expound, explicate, or interpret; technical term for commentary or exegesis of the Holy Qur'an.
ʿulamā (sing. *ʿālim*): scholars.
Ummāh: faith community, nation.

www.ingramcontent.com/pod-product-compliance
Ingram Content Group UK Ltd.
Pitfield, Milton Keynes, MK11 3LW, UK
UKHW022241230426
12048UKWH00018BA/1393